Hail fellow, most well met!

Well Met:
Poems of Companionship

by Joffre Swait

Joffre Swait *Well Met: Poems of Companionship*
© 2017 by Joffre Swait

Published by Jovial Press, 2106 E. 63rd, Spokane, WA 99223
www.jovial-pub.com
Printed in the United States of America

17 18 19 20 21 22   9 8 7 6 5 4 3 2 1

ISBN: 1-68411-450-0
ISBN-13: 978-1-68411-450-4

TO MY FATHER

I went to sail upon the sea
Of mankind's discontent,
But all I saw was a fishin' hole
By which I pitched my tent.

I came near to its sandy shores,
And was left, well, quite befuddled.
That which I'd thought a vasty sea
Was less than a pond, 't'was a puddle.

I stripped my clothes, not to be daunted,
And dove headlong headfirst…
And found, very much to my chagrin,
The world had been reversed.

I dove in hard, led with my head,
Expecting to hit ground,
But a chasm as deep as Marianas
Was the only thing I found.

I gazed into that briny deep,
Awaiting demons bitter;
But all I saw was two sad shades
Approach me all a-jitter.

In ghostly form they floated to me,
All trembley and all pale,
And said, as Robert Zimmerman would,
"It's not a sea, it's a jail!"

"It's true this sea of discontent
Is deep and wordly wide.
It would take ten thousand years
To reach the other side."

"There's plenty that you could explore
If you ever so desired,
But after the first million years
Of boredom you'd be tired."

I realized then that what they'd said
Was true as true could be,
And that I'd known it well before
I'd dived into this sea.

"It's best to not so introspect
Such interest in myself;
A gainful study of mankind
Is made in other books upon the shelf."

I climbed out of the puddle
And headed back downtown
To see if any childhood friends
Were still trolling around.

The town was empty, the lights all off,
No soul disturbed the dark,
Except my dad, in simple calm
On a bench out in the park.

"Son," he said, "I'm glad you're back,
I really wasn't sure
If you'd stop being self-obsessed
And listening to The Cure."

"You thought this town was a dead end
Where life would be cut short;
Listen for once to crazy dad:
This town's made a spaceport."

"The town entire's gone astronaut,
(And I'm not far behind)
To explore the astral fields and fires,
To go new worlds find."

"I told you that we'd take this trip
Years ago, it seems.
Instead it looks like you forgot
And turned to Puddle Dreams."

"I gave you this when you were young,
In fact, you were just two.
I never said what it was for,
But I said what it would do."

He stepped forward and he hugged me,
And dropped it in my pocket.
I pulled it out as he walked away:
A key to my own rocket.

I looked closely and inscribed I saw
Bright words upon the key,
A nursery rhyme that now made sense,
Which he had read to me:

"This is the key of the kingdom.
In that kingdom there is a city.
In that city there is a street.
In that street there is a yard.
In that yard there is a house.
In that house there is a room.
In that room there is a bed.
By that bed there is a basket.
In that basket there are some flowers.
Flowers in the basket,
Basket by the bed,
Bed in the room,
Room in the house,
House in the yard,
Yard in the street,
Street in the city,
City in the kingdom,
And this is the key of the kingdom."

FOREWORD

There is an Old English word that ought to be revived. *Ge-beárscipe* would transliterate to 'beership.' It is the fellowship of people drinking beer together. Or more specifically people drinking beer, telling stories, and reciting poetry together. Wouldn't it be wonderful to have a word at hand to describe such a scene. Of course, such a scene would need to be recovered as well, since this kind of fellowship is rare, but perhaps the recovery of the word will aid in the recovery of the fellowship.

The truth of the matter is that our thoughtless use of matter is the problem. God gave us stuff, and as C.S. Lewis quipped, he must like it. He gave us a lot of it. But we do not seem to have a grasp on what it is for. We use it day in and day out, in support of life and limb. We eat, drink, and breathe matter in order to stay alive, yet we never seem to wonder if there is more to it. But in God's economy, matter is given to us as a means of fellowship. Too many meals are eaten by people all facing the same direction. We get our energy package #3 with no onions and a Dr. Pepper from a window and consume it on the way to our next event. And while the food and drink might reach our waistlines (praise God whose glory is weighty), the food and drink never reach their telos, the purpose for which they were created.

God created the stuff of the world for fellowship. We were clay-made as hungry creatures in an edible world so that we could feed one another. So that we could be knit into one another in the act of eating and drinking together. We were given limbs and legs so that we could dance together, becoming brothers and sisters in new and creative ways. Husbands and wives have two bodies of flesh so that they could laugh and cry and love and, in the two-flesh-tangle, could tango into one. It is a story of glory multiplying as one and one become one. With the power in this passionate companionship being such that entirely new people pop into existence through the camaraderie.

Matter is made for fellowship. God gave beer so that beership could bring us together and in bringing us together, bring Him glory. God gave bread so that companionship could be enjoyed. The etymology of companionship is, after all, 'joined with the sharing of bread.' God gave matter so that it could get between us as a point of contact. Gifts, toasts, and shared pleasures bring matter to its intended end.

Hoarded pleasures rot the soul. Pleasures shared enlarge it.

Even our bodies are made of matter so that we can come together. Men have hands so that they can shake them in greeting, high five, and embrace one another in masculine affection. Husbands have arms so that they can hold their wives and dance with them in front of a sink full of suds. They have fingers and thumbs so that they can rub their wives feet at the end of the day, and beards so that they can tickle the cricks and napes of their wives joints. Wives have bodies. And that is simply enough to say, since I have not the words to describe the way my heart leaps within me to think of the ensorcelling fellowship that matter—formed into the body of a woman —can enflame when she knows she is safe and cherished. Matter is given by God so that it can be given and received and shared. So that we, as people made in the Image of God, can know the unknowable mysteries of the life of the Father, Son, and Holy Spirit.

But how might I quit treating people as objects? How might I, instead, begin to use the objects in my life to connect with the people around me? You could do worse than beginning with this collection of poetry. There is a balanced, yet enthusiastic embrace of the world that Swait finds at hand. With a fanatic eagerness in the enjoyment of wife, hearth, guest, and table, Joffre is a competent guide in the embrace of the world God made. He can show you how to do it. And you will not be able to keep from enjoying the view as Swait, with his jolly bear hug of the native strengths of her rhythms and her sounds, puts his large and hairy arms around the waist of the English language and takes her out to the dance floor.

You were made for joy and eternal fellowship. Let *Well Met* lead you down out of the balcony of your life so that you can rejoin the party.

Jason Farley
Jovial Hall, Spokane
Autumnal Equinox, 2017 AD

CONTENTS

DOGGEREL

Ave Atque Vale
I meet a friend after work

Hail fellow, most well met,
I slap thee on the back and shoulder!
Here's ale bowls for thee to wet
Thy throat and whistle before you get older.
Long hast labored, and hast sweat;
Drink thou this beer, it gets no colder.
Then get thee hence, all free from debt,
Thy kids to kiss, thy wife, to hold her.

A Busy Year For Spain

In 1492 Columbus sailed the ocean blue.
'Twas also the year the Inquisitor kicked out the Jew.
Oh, they slew the Caliphs too.

Jack The Giant-Killer

There once was a boy named Jack
Who had a peculiar knack.
He'd made quite a science
Out of skewering giants
And piling their heads up in stacks.

Saint Augustine

This Hippan just couldn't understand
How natural was evil in man.
With his friends he did loot
A pear tree of its fruit;
The motive was "just 'cause we can".

Why St. Nick Has Red Cheeks

Old Nicholas of Myra was fat
And wore an extremely tall hat.
He gave out his treats
To kids in bare feets,
And drank his red wine by the vat.

I'm a Man Who Enjoys Some Strong Rye

I'm a man who enjoys some strong rye,
For it makes me both happy and spry.
Though whiskey is brown
In country and town,
It is best when it's mud in your eye.

There Once was a Boy Named George

There once was a boy named George
Who every morning ate porridge.
One day he rebelled
And loudly he yelled:
"Bring meat, not these grasses and forage!"

MEANT TO AMUSE

Learning Not To Challenge Movie Buffs
In Which A Poser Is Exposed

If a chicken and duck had sat down and ate,
And spoke about breadcrumbs and weather, and all,
When talk settled on how one might migrate,
The chicken's opinion would be thought very small.

If you find yourself sitting outside, drinking joe,
With a film buff of citywide fame and repute,
And talk turns from Augustine's concept of soul
To which actor starred in that Brit action shoot,

Behoove you it would to keep your mouth closed.
The last thing you'd do, if at all you were wise,
Would be place a bet, since you'd likely get hosed
And taught a hard lesson by more sensible guys.

A chicken knows less than a duck of migration,
And roosters know more about crowing.
But the fool will step beyond his due station,
And challenge the sage in his tower of knowing.

Manna & Quail

"You shall eat until it comes out at your nostrils."
Numbers 11:18-22

Lord, all men must feed on words,
and poetry is our grain.
In a land that grows only wild rice
we ask for farms and rain.

Give us limericks for the happy times
and sonnets for the hot.
Give us meter when the forecast's good
but free verse when it's not.

Billy Collins is nice in the morning,
Eliot's for the afternoon;
Lewis or Hopkins are good with tea,
Kipling with an immense monsoon.
But O Lord,
for your name and mercy's sake,
never give us William Blake.

If heavenly words are to be our diet,
there's all sorts of poetry,
and we'd like to try it.
But oh! lest our menu be all prose,
please, please Lord, please,
let not our poetry come out of our nose.

Batter My Heart
A Son Asks For Breakfast

Batter this griddle, thrice-blesséd mom; for, you
As yet but beat, sift, stir, mix the leaven,
That it may rise, stand, puff nicely to heaven;
So cook, and if it burn make it new.
I, like a besiegéd town, without my vittles,
Labour to patience, but oh, to no use.
Ham, and biscuit, coffee, orange juice,
Make me crave sorely; so dear woman, please griddle!
Dearly I love you, and would love to wait,
Yet am undone by the aroma of bacon.
So pour that batter, flip it onto a plate.
Soon brothers and sisters will smell what you're makin'.
I beg you to stack them in piles at least three,
I will never be fed unless you will feed me.

the song of osteen

a true-life interview by stephen colbert done in the style of don marquis' archy

this is the song of osteen
the song of osteen
of osteen the alley cat
the song of osteen
as i wrote you before viewers
osteen is a believer
in the pythagorean
theory of the transmigration
of blessing and he claims
that formerly his spirit
was incarnated in the body
of the image of victory
that was obviously a big deal
and one must not be
surprised if osteen
has forgotten some of his
more subtle manners

i am the colbert
who has a radiovision show
and i host the greatest
prophets and believers of the age
i am myself a prophet somewhat
and one day i popped my
typewriter and announced
i am going to write a song
the song of osteen
of osteen the alley cat
and i will host

the song of osteen
i will write it
on my radiovision show
i am just a cockroach
with a typewriter
osteen is an alleycat
with a football stadium

i know that i am bound
for a journey down the sound
in the midst of a refuse mound
a friend once said
and i must heartily concur
wotthehell whotthehell

when he came to my set
wotthehell whotthehell

he said two words
that will change your life
which are buy this book
which immediately explained
his trinitarian thought
because that is not only two words
but another two words were
I AM like the books name
the power of I AM

moses and the burning bush
i said that seems like a lot
like a mystery
like what more do you have
to add to the word of God

mine is a different take on it
a happier different take on it
what follows I AM is
what we invite into our lives
for example i am
toujours gai toujours gai
it changed how oprah saw her life

so this is the power
i said
of positive
but i hesitated
of positiv
vvvvvv
vvv
vvvvision
for yourself
i said

the power in our words
is i think people dont realize
how many times
we speak negative things
about ourselves

i do that all the time
i said
im so stupid

oh thats so funny
the osteens teeth glared
everyone laughed

do you have to believe in Jesus
to read this book

no
cuz jesus went outside the box
if you are outside the box
i will still talk to you
was the great alley cats
implication or is it suggestion
i have been a little
unusual he said
i talk about life and forgiveness
these are themes
untouched inside the box
other prophets never say
life and forgiveness
also i say
good attitudes
reach dreams
a lot of times
a lot of times
religion pushes people down

ten millions people
cats and cockroaches
and a verisimilitude of
other creatures thats a lot
of other creatures
tune into your radiovision
prophecies i said
thats as big as some religions

like i said he said
i have been a little unusual
i have gone outside
the box
there are so many alleys
for an alley cat
but religion pushes people down
the power of I AM
is what follows after
having good attitudes

as a catholic cockroach
i must ask have you tried
the power of crushing guilt

oh thats so funny
people say to me
im guilty enough
so i dont go to church
our message is a little bit
different god is for you

is there one thing
one prophet to another
is there one thing
a core message
that is not one of prosperity
is there one thing
to take from this book
i asked with precision

to which responded
to wit wotthehell wotthehell

osteen the alley cat
dont be against yourself
i am the image of God
i am a masterpiece
recall that i am
a believer
in the pythagorean
theory of the transmigration
of blessing and
that formerly my spirit
was incarnated in the body
of the image of victory
that was obviously a big deal
quit being against yourself
i am fearfully and wonderfully
made im strong and talented

one prophet to another
i said
from one prophet
you are obviously
strong and talented
plus you seem like you have abs

oh thats so funny
thank you for having me colbert
the cockroach

Homemade Sausage
A Poem About Marriage

A plump wife loves her sausage well,
And loves with generous ardor,
But only if you keep her shelf
And cupboard fully lardered.

As every maiden chaste well knows,
It's best to marry a man of the land.
He'll be good when he plows, sure when he sows,
And know how to handle her lusty demands.

A salumista's daughter married
The salt of the earth, a farmer's son.
And once she over the threshold was carried
He learned what a prize of a woman he'd won.

"I have skill beyond a normal bride's,"
She said as he put her down.
"My father's delight, when my mother had fried
His sausage just right, could be heard 'round the town.

"When I came of age my mother's instruction
On how to make bangers I heeded full well.
Her recipes all on sausage production
I'm eager to try if you'll lay down a spell.

"The men in this county all talk without end.
It's butchers, and pigs, and who's biggest herd.
But now that I've come, seen the size of your pens,
You've got so much meat it's almost absurd.

"Yes, a plump wife loves her sausage well,
And loves with generous ardor,
But only if you keep her shelf
And cupboard fully lardered.

"I can make you kielbasa, just like the Poles.
I'll smoke it for days, the tenderest meat.
I'll squeeze it and grind it, then press into rolls.
The pop and the spurt when you bite is a treat.

"I'll make you paprika chorizo with chili,
Just as spicy and hot as you can bear.
Taste the fire I've got, the ride burns your tongue silly,
And a few hours later the spice is still there.

"Speaking of spice, and the meat that you own,
The steps for andouille are simple to do.
A more salut'ry sausage has never been known,
The fat makes you strong, and the wine well will too.

"When a hot dog or wiener's made simply and right,
Just know you'll be pleased that I know how to bake.
Slide it into my bun and take a big bite,
With a bit of the relish from pickles I make.

"Yes, my relish will prove it's true:
I'm good with cucumber too."

"Better's the wurst when times have been hard,
Just give me one hog, I'll be happy and filled.
For even bologna, with its cubes of pressed lard
Is healthful and tasty when seasoned with skill.

"Marriage, my husband, is an oath and a pledge,
With contracts and duties for wife and for man.
Be sure every day tend my garden and hedge,
Trim the bushes all regular to keep me in hand.

"For the times that are lean I'll make winter salami;
If you must be up early it will be chipolata.
For the times that are easy a sausage romani;
If you'd like times of quiet I can make soppressata,

"A plump wife loves her sausage well,
And loves with generous ardor,
But only if you keep her shelf
And cupboard fully lardered.

"For I delight in sausage, and you delight in me,
And if you give me sausage, I will delight in thee.

"So go you out from home each day,
Give me all the meat you breed.
When you return at night to lay,
You'll know your farmer's seed
Has taken hold with winsome worth:
And yet more sausage-makers will walk upon this earth."

As you can imagine the farmer was pleased
To hear such a speech from his spouse,
They held on to each other until they released,
Professing their faith by shaking the house.

LESS THAN EPIC

Florida Freeway Haiku

When we hit the Indiantown
exit going south,
heat lightning out to sea.

Waiting For Your Birthday

The best poems about mothers
Feature specific and evocative episodes.
For example, the time I wanted to eat
The plastic fruit at the Orange Julius,
Or the time you sent me to the barber alone
And I came back with a mohawk.

But this is not a poem about you.
It is about me, because I leave this here
Expecting something back.

Which reminds me of being eight,
On this day years ago.
It was your birthday,
And all the kids got new bikes.

A Homeschooler Remembers His Mother

You made me memorize three poems.
"Why do you say, O Jacob, and complain, O Israel", and
"Now I will show you a more excellent way", and
"The quality of mercy is not strained".
Even now, twenty years removed,
These three abide.

When at the last you left me alone
I read whatever I wanted.
But if I teach the kids a family history,
Or if they try to find reasons to skip math,
I see you through a glass darkly.
And if I speak in the tongues of
The Abridged Shakespeare Company,
Or the pastor preaches a sermon on love,
Blessing both him that gives and him that receives,
I think of the year I finally
And regrettably
Tired.

Even youths grow tired and weary
And young men stumble and fall.

I think sometimes about
Then we shall see face to face,
But mostly I think
If I prick you
You will not bleed.

The Strongest Peoples of Earth Are the Free
On The Longbow

Not 'til full metal jackets
came around
would this sort of firepower
be matched.

This was a peculiar fire
(its verb "to loose"),
a rain
of wood and steel
and each drop
from up high
a full yard long.

At a rate of, what,
seven, eight a minute.
Bolt-action rifles bettered that easily
half a millennium later.

Napoleon's columns could not stand up
to the thin lines
of the quickest army of his age.
Those early sons of Welsh and Cornish villagers
could manage only four shots a minute.

Crossbowmen from Genoa
were more precise, (so Latin),
but much slower (also).

One English shaft could punch
halfway through a church door
and popped (like rain on a tin roof)
through the knights in their full metal jackets.

Ben Franklin was a wise man
(early to bed)
but perhaps his most immortal insight
was to say how much earlier
our war would have been won
by an army of longbowmen.

The French and Scots had a few,
of course, but in England it was a national sport.
For a couple of centuries, that made the difference.
You can't just train that into a man
in a few months.
It's a lifelong endeavor.

Wellington owed his victories
to the playing fields of Eton,
but Edward to Sunday afternoon contests.
Practice, practice, practiced
in pulling a six-foot longbow.
I mean, imagine the shoulders.
Sport was the turning point of Western Europe.
and by the time a law was made
to practice every Sunday it was too late.

All good Englishmen need their day of rest,
and the strongest peoples of earth are the free.

God Eats

Stephen was delicious because he was beaten,
tenderized by many stones,
his forgiveness-kneaded flesh
softened by killing blows.

Sharper than any butcher's cleaver
is the Word of God,
living and active,
piercing to the division of joints and marrow.
When finally pierced
between soul and spirit
he was made to be a perfect meal.

His God was a consuming fire
who devoured all his apostles
with delight, and smelled the smoke
of their burning as a sweet aroma.
Only their outsides were charred
as on a grill or cast-iron.
Their flesh was rare and easily cut.

Andrew and Peter were hung
upside down like pheasants,
left to age until perfect.
This is not to everyone's taste,
but monks and martyrs recommend it.

Paul was a work of art,
stricken, smitten, and afflicted,
tenderized several times.
On one single trip he was

marinated,
slow-cooked,
and injected with a fiery seasoning
designed to amaze.
Dry-aged then for two years
he was finally drained
and offered up quietly
without much to-do,
just as the sophisticates like it.
This is an excellent way
to prepare an older animal.

Only to a privileged few
does it fall
to be cooked over direct flame.
Most of us, like Paul, are allowed to get old.
Too old,
or perhaps it is simply a divine preference for brisket.

For your sake we are cooked
all the day long
in a little wine
which will finally break down
the tougher-habited sinews.
It's been a long time coming

But soon the great fork of God
will make your flesh
to fall tenderly off your bones,
the provings past,
the tastings done,
and you, served up
perfect.

Artistic Appropriation

In Homage To The Cover Of C. S. Lewis'
        "Poems," 1992, Harcourt Brace & Co.

The angel bore Saint George's cross
And stood 'midst clouds on cherubs' heads.
To remind them all of Ocean's loss
Old Jove sailed by the Moon's dry beds.
And when the mighty angel knew
The horse's myth-begetting corn,
He spread his wings (shine every hue!),
A blast he blew upon his horn:

For all this thank we Photoshop.

Plundering The Egyptians
Eating The World's Art

The rivers of Babylon flow, and fall, and bear away,
But Zion is holy, every thing firm, and no thing falls.

By rivers sit we, not under nor in them, but from above;
Not standing nor upright, but humble and seated, yet from
    above.

Thus stand we on porches in David's throne city, nothing
    falls.
Let us see if the pleasure is firm or fleeting: shall we bear it
    away?

Freedom in Form

In those days of sweater vests,
When men wore hats,
And children ties
With the top button cinched.

In those days without tennis shoes
Except for exercise,
In those days of *yes ma'am*
And *no ma'am* and get up
When she walks in.

In those days of closed air,
In that ancient day of rules
At work, at home, at play;

In those days of always deference,
When life was shorter, shorter and tighter;
In those days a man could light his pipe,
Or not, as he wished.

The World Is Too

I have the books to prove
I am a serious history buff.

Discovering my mother's ancestors
were Russian Jews surprised me
and you know how I loved my mother.
I can think of only two Hank Williams songs
off the top of my head, but I definitely remember
the name of his hometown
unless I am actually driving through south Alabama.

Frivolous were the romantics and shallow Wordsworth,
but I can't recall the titles to any of his poems
except the world is too much with us.

So what if I see great Proteus rise from the sea
or hear old Triton on the horn
with those whose names are never called
when choosing sides for basketball?

I am making coffee mixed with epic butter,
which is not a thing people did
in my father's time.

I want to be a man who says
It is not that I am unmoved. Great God! No.
It is still tomorrow the waking up,
if given a new creed I might have sight
to make me less forlorn, but that is not the problem.

The difficulty in moving the piano
way down the wave
is not its weight, nor even the time of mistakes.

It's that the thing is too big
and will not fit through my heart.

Family Photos

Your smile is a reward
Is what I meant to say
When I said you never smiled
As much as your brother.

Ego

I am self-consciously poetic.
Which is usually a little awkward,
Like the girl at the end of a romance
Who says, "Wouldn't this be the perfect end to my novel?"
It's affected, contrived, but gratifying.

Take, for example, the other day,
When I used a glass-bottle soda cap as an ashtray,
Left it on the coffeeshop table.
I would feel let down if I discovered that
The person who sat down after me
Failed to write a poem about my little ashtray.

Beginning With the Logos (A Sonnet for Advertising)

Un soneto d'amore per G. M. Hopkins e Wendell Berry

The Roman roads endure, and English trails
Still cut through Appalachians, axe and Indian.
How great are man's achieves, the engines and rails:
The whiskey-fueled Burmese, the grand Canadian.
But greatest yet, the wide and open flow
Of six-lane American brand-name roads,
Of neon, of franchise, and plastic signs in a row.
Beginning with the logos, enfleshed in gold,
These wide and brazen paths, all lit at night
Drown the stars above and block the trees;
But not one name, or center, or communal site,
Is known. All sprawled are the places we take our ease.
The tributary streets do not meet, but fall,
Separate, downtownless, to drink the malls.

The Death of Romance

*A Poem in Excerpts From the Middle Ages to Today, Found at the
Foot of a Tower of Song*

Childe Rowland to the dark tower came.

My Lord Cid Don Rodrigo
Straight for the gateway made.
And they that held it when they saw
That swift attack fled in great fear.

Unto the foot of the tower we came at last.

Then came Arthur out of his tower
And had under his gown a jesseraunt
Of double mail, and went with him
The Archbishop of Canterbury.

Lo! Yonder is (said she) the brazen tower!

Those are not giants, they are windmills.
Before that ruin came, for centuries
Tough men-at-arms, cross-gartered to the knees
Or shod in iron, climbed the narrow stairs.

That night three unsuccessful bombing attacks
Were made on the Tower at Wancourt.

I wait for Childe Roland
To come to the final darkest tower.
I wait for Aphrodite.

Across the River To Another Life

In the offshoots of the Suwannee
The river-trees debate.
Is it nobler in the mind
(If you *must* fall
And be in clear shallow waters
Sticking out a bit):
Is it better for three turtles
To sun on you in a neat line
As carp swim by,
Or would you rather
Be moss covered in the shade,
One single yellow flower up
And alive in your hollowed-out barque?

Concentration

I have to be careful still
when I bring up the braces
you were wearing on the day we met.
Though I tell everyone we know
behind your back.

You wore undignified overalls
- because you oil-painted your studies -
not caring if you looked like a little kid.
Your classmates' ruffled artist outfits
were more carefully considered.

Is it adorable still
that I thought your soteriology sexy,
or that we stopped to talk with tiny winged giraffes
on our off-campus walks?

Is it cute or creepy when I relate the story
of how I told you we'd get married
and you told me to get lost?
Instead I called you at three every morning.

For your senior project
I was your husband the elephant,
you a hedgehog.
Your classmates thought we were into S & M.

That was hard work, that year
probably harder than the babies
that followed, five of the best
and none seemed to get any easier.
You not painting.

The house you wanted
for the lawn you said,
then built yourself more
garden for every year.

The shop we opened you loved so much.
Its failure. We began to count
the years by which cats we adopted,
which died.

You had your braces removed
at age eighteen, although they did nothing
to fix your teeth being small like a little kid's,
and now our third boy has your teeth.

Your concentration then was
hard to look away from,
- your babyface and exploded hair
bent over a canvas -
I wanting you to look at me as intently.

I wrote you youthful poetry,
which you said was flattering
and you thought was nice,
that you remember none of today.

Which is why, right now, you are completely unaware
that when you concentrate still
you look exactly like those poems.

All The Things I Know About Women
An erotic poem

Every woman's hips are gold,
their bellies made of fire.
And if their thighs to touch you're bold,
there's more gold to desire.

Every woman's hair is shined
like precious beaten metal,
And flies around her head to bind
your eyes to golden vessel.

Every woman's haunch is rounded
soft but filled with strength to carry;
Their feet are small and light the ground
to dance and to make merry.

A woman's breasts are fulsome land
of youth and life and plenty.
They delight the eye and fill the hand
and feed you 'til they're empty.

Each woman's fawns are bright and new,
and pinkly when you meet,
Then ripen to a wine-like hue
to drunk you with their sweet.

Only once a woman's young,
lean in maidenhood.
If you find her in your hunts,
you've found what's very good.

And every woman older blooms
with laugh lines and with children.
Her house of love will add on rooms
and soon become a mansion.

Of women I've had every taste,
the virgin and the matron.
Some were lusty, some were chaste
With sexy little aprons.

I've never had an old old woman,
but that's all right, I'm patient.
I've heard they're built like trees to heaven,
all wrinkled, strong, and gracious.

Every woman builds your hearth,
and every woman makes.
Every woman breaks your heart,
and every woman takes.

I know the things I've said are true
of every living Eve,
'Cause every one I ever knew
was kind to've married me.

I've only known the single one,
we've had a crop of kids.
I knew her when we both were young,
and since, we've broken beds.

I met her when she'd braces on,
with cutesome overalls;
I told her that the chase was on,
and that I was enthralled.

From her I've learned why women laugh,
their sorrows and their labors.
If they're all like the one I have
we'd all best beg their favor.

If you will wonder at their loves
and wander all their beauties:
Then cup her towers and kiss her doves
and give her many babies.

A woman's breasts are a fulsome land
of youth and life and plenty.
They delight the eye and fill the hand
and feed you 'til they're empty.

How Like A God

Looking down on a new city
from a third-story restaurant
is not like being a god
in the sense that I am on top of the world,

it is like being a god
in the sense that I am
better than you,
that I am judging you in this moment,
oh motorcycle pizza delivery guy,
seen from above
through a canopy of flowers,
playing with a colleague's son.

Not judging in the sense
of heaven and hell,
but in the sense of the senses.
I am deciding that your moment
on the sidewalk immediately below me
is beautiful
and that I am worthy to say it is so.

Also this is like being a god
in the sense that I am independent of you,
completely other.

I am sure I understand you
Even though you do not even see me
and could never hope to understand
from down there, without revelation
that is,

if I were not completely condescending
in the theological sense.

A City Tree Is An Elegant Tree

There's elegance in a small pale tree
That grows from its specially selected
Department of Urban Development site,
With a half-foot trunk growing
Through a grate peculiarly designed for it.
Such a tree displays latent bonsaism,
And its middle trunk will show the earholes
Left by long-gone limbs.
Its top branches will be like a spinster aunt's hair,
Sticking out a little wild,
But not presuming to take up too much space.
The trimmers will not need to visit a tree like that very
    often,
Because it is elegant, a graceful tree.
And elegance is content in her station.

Theobroma
A beer review

Remarkable
Was what you pronounced,
Which seemed to go without saying,
Given that you'd remarked upon it.

Still, something had to be said.
The way the light shone through
The cloudy deep orange of the thing.
The crisp bubbly of the day,
How well it matched the bright.

Still something more had to be said
Of the fresh face it gave to age,
How your job seemed manageable,
And your spirit was content in its dispensations.

Remarkable,
You said.
I poured another.

Life Before The Internet

For our memories
of how it was before
they will despise us.

The last generation before
will tell its stories
but they will say
do you mean it was like
when we are children?
Was it a slow waking
awareness?

And their children in turn will say
is it like when you are dead,
or before you ever were?

Curse of Womb
Hosea 9

Our friends' necks
are outstretched,
our neighbors
plot against us.
They have served
their belly-
god of fire,
coming down
from killing
their babies.
They tip off
policemen,
kindly seize
our children.
Where is he.
Thunder is
His voice but
where is he?
An abundance
of horses.

Their dust shall
cover us.
Our walls shake
at the noise
of horsemen,
of chariots.
I make thee
desolate.
He said that.

Ephraim
is smitten,
from the birth,
from the womb,
even from
conception.
Like a bird
our glory
flies away.

To Baal-Peor
wanton rites,
homicides
to Moloch.
We bring up
our children,
But he
bereaves us.

We bring forth
our children,
planted in
pleasant place,
to murders.
Give us, Lord.
What wilst give?
Miscarrying
womb, dry breasts.
Roots dried up,
bear not fruit.
We bring forth,
He will slay.
Even fruit,

beloved
fruit of womb.

Policemen
kindly seize
our children,
voice is heard
in Ramah,
Belly god
consumes them
because us,
because we
climbed the heights,
sacred trees,
and played whore.

Our friends' necks
plot against us.
We shall be
wanderers
among them
the nations,
Till he save
till he save
till he saves us.

Thrice Beaten With Rods, And Baked Into Bread
ἦθος ἀνθρώπῳ δαίμων

Is this the body and the blood for real
Or do I eat by sweat of wrinkled brow?
Feed on doubt and lust even as I kneel?

The words were spoken plain and bare as steel
But I would rate and complicate them now.
Is this the body and the blood for real?

There is no magic done to see or feel
Except a spelling of words in a woven vow.
I feed on doubt and lust even as I kneel.

Nor art nor philosophy make of it a meal
That does what's solemnly said. He never told how
This is the body and the blood for real.

Maybe it's animal weakness for social congeal,
The sodded quick of boiled bones' marrow
Where stew the doubt and lust even as I kneel.

But under this red rock is the new deal.
Not under; this rock's the whole loaf now.
It is the body and the blood for real,
Again I feed on bread and wine, and kneel.

The Peace of Bees

Bees are the bug
To write poems about.
Bees are the bug
To describe all the things.
Bees are the bug
Who flit in and out.
Bees are the bug
Whom out from truth rings.

Bees are the bug
About whom it could be said
The buzz of bees
The busy of bees
The business of bees.
Also it could be said
The work of bees
The love of bees
The devotion of bees,
Even the peace.

Bees are the bugs
Who work for others,
And bees are the bugs
Who love you.

Gospel Resolve

It's over the every-morning coffee
that you notice the blood-red sun
of every day and it's over
the commuter steering wheel
that you see the angels' stair
of every day and it's over
the flickering fluorescent
and the xerox machine
that you realize

Tomorrow I will sip
at a fresh cup of coffee
your wife will pour for me
before sitting beside you
with her small glass of white grape juice.

After we speak the speech
of every day and it's over
we will arise, we three
we will walk out your open door
into an apocalyptic everyday morning,
and we shall beat our kings into plowshares
our swords into gardeners.

EPIC

The Faithfulness of Images (Ceci n'est pas une pipe)
Numbers 25 retold for the contemporary art world

Most artists suffer from worldly malaise,
They feel they've got to get out of this place:
If it's the last thing they ever do,
If it takes selling old cans of their poo.

The meaning of things, if read like they're plain,
Points to a truth, and that'd be insane.
So a pipe's not a pipe, it must be a peter,
And if you write poems there must be no meter.

I'll tell you a story, but change it a titch,
So it will be modern, and relevant, and *sic.*
The Lay of Young Phinehas, now that's a good story,
Although at the end it gets a bit gory:

At Shittim in Moab was a colony of arts;
It attracted all of the Moabite tarts.
They called out to every Israelite male:
"Come on, don't be so uptight and stale."

"The thing these days is to play the whore
And bow down before the Baal of Peor.
Our philosophy is one that makes life a feast,
We'll party with all, be they man, be they beast.

"We're most surprised at all of you Jews,
For haven't you heard the latest good news?
'Nothing is real', the Walrus hath said.
Life is a beach, then you are dead.

"Our art is subjective, and so is our sex,
And we've found that it has no ill side-effects.
So come on, young dude, into my tent,
And we'll party as if 't'were the day before Lent."

So the sons of the Jews decided to orgy,
And sent many thousands to lie in the morguey.
(*De mortuis*, I know, it really is shocking.
I mean really, this rhyming's a little too mocking.)

The elders then spoke: "It has to stop now!
This evil has killed full twenty-four thou."
They put out an edict, a strong-word command:
"Return to the faithful God of your land."

Well, some of 'em did, but some of 'em did'n'ianite,
And one of the rebels took him a Midianite.
He brought her in front of the Tent of the Meeting:
"I'm going to get pleasure, for this life is fleeting."

That Israelite took her right into his house,
And was doing with her what you do with a spouse.
But Phinehas, he thrust a spear through their bellies,
Right after their bowels with fear turned to jellies.

The rebel's last words had been very clear.
"Dude," he told Phinehas, "that isn't a spear.
Meaning's subjective, a pipe's not a pipe,
And that phallic symbol is really just tripe."

Phinehas then: "That's an old tune, that song.
But soon you will know my spear's six feet long.
The flint-tip is real, so this is the day
I'll circ'cise your heart in a literal way."

Most artists suffer from what is called *ennui*.
They hurry to bid their cheerless lives *bon nuit*.
"Nothing is real", the Walrus has said.
Life is a bitch, then they are dead.

Yes, Christians when writing are prone to use simile
(Now we see in a mirror but dimile).
Metaphors are great, and so is a symbol.
Without them we'd sound like resounding...uh...cymbals.

The waffle is a symbol I know to hate,
It oozes its weakness all over my plate.
Much more my style is something like wine,
Which serves me as blood, and seems to work fine.

The Lesson Man Learns, or Else He Fries:
God never lies.

Why Men Should Not Wear Skimpy Bathing Suits

Everyone likes to talk 'bout *Il Duce*,
How Italy had places to go.
But his generals, they wore turkey feathers and Gucci,
And declined to face a tough foe.

It's difficult, when picking a fight,
With nations to south and to north,
If your soldiers wear loafers so light
And mince-step when sallying forth.

I realize it's been covered before,
I know it's a well-worn theme:
How *Italia* wore the dress of a whore,
Which, when tugged at, ripped at the seam.

Her martial men have been flogged,
Their reputation now has a stench.
The bright shield of Priam's been fogged;
Why, they've even been compared to the French!

What lots of people don't know,
What's evaded the average reader:
Her armed forces weren't all leavened dough,
There was one corps made proud its leader!

In Africa, at night, the tankers would run
Full tilt right into the trees.
On patrol the pilots would look at the sun
To find Spitfires coming in threes.

But of one thing papa and mama were proud
While chewing their gnocci in gravy.
There was a force fascist that yet was unbowed:
The illustrious Italian Navy!

British Tars, who're named for the combative lime,
Have a fine reputation for ruling the sea.
But *Il Duce*, that fiend, with his force maritime,
Would pick off their convoys, and spit in their tea.

The Brits had been left solitaire in the Med,
Quite suddenly, and yes, 't'was a shock.
The French fleet, once allied, went Vichy instead,
Leaving Limey alone on the Rock.

The Admiralty put all of their heads close together,
Deciding to think of a plot
That, God willing (that is, and the weather)
Would pull them right out of this spot.

"*Toujours, toujours, toujours l'audace!*"
Said they, without any flim-flummery.
"If we don't succeed, it will be our pink arse,
Plus we'll lose Montgomery's army!"

Six Latin warships made Taranto their port,
Just before Britain turned there to strike.
Some Saxons would look on Valhalla's bright court,
Some Romans would see what Elysium was like.

As far as raids go, this one was quite neat,
With ten different task forces sailing around.
Some came from Malta, some came straight from Crete,
And this criss-crossing did the Italians confound.

Then that great carrier, *Illustrious* by name,
Launched all of her Swordfish, loaded for bear.
And to the Italians ne'er dying shame
Those two dozen biplanes bearded them in their lair.

Fascist inventory listed: "Full Battleships, Six,"
Which made the Med *Mare Nostrum*.
But when the English flyers were done with their tricks
The Italians had all *Mare* lostum.

The lesson we've learnt from this short naval history:
That men of some nations wear speedos,
But others leave much more to mystery...
Those nations with bigger torpedoes.

Thanksgiving Poems

For Public Performances

The God of Pumpkin Pie

The beasts of the forest all thank God in chorus
For the acorns all strewn 'neath the light of the moon.

The oak tree is king in the woods of the East,
Its roots reach down deep to the sky.
A flock of plump turkey passing through make their feast,
On thèm we'll the same with a sigh!
We'll eat turkey and pumpkin pie, my boys,
Turkey and pumpkin pie!

The boar roots and snuffles, the sow digs the truffles.
For the treats that they find they thank God who is kind.

The pigs whom we feed and tender our care
As there in their wallows they lie,
Are sweetest of meat and súrpassing fair
When cured off the rib and the thigh.
So it's ham and pumpkin pie, my boys,
Ham and pumpkin pie!

The beasts of the bog, the Boggart, the Frog,
And magical Man, how they love berry cran.

The woodpeckers, warblers, and wrens of the slew
Never thought in their time 'neath the sky
To mix sweet and tart in a red gummy goo
That the Maker of all glorifies.
So it's sauce and pumpkin pie, my boys!
Sauce and pumpkin pie!

The brewster or brewer, that fat barley stewer
Lifts hands up to heaven for grain and for leaven!

Of saints for all ales, either brewed or mirác'lous,
The church she has never been shy.
Even good old Saint Nick, and Saint Arnold the maculate,
Praised our Gód for unending supply!
So it's beer and pumpkin pie, my boys!
Beer and pumpkin pie!

You creatures of God, who dwell on the sod
You armies above, to your dread Lord in love,
From whom blessings flow to the high and the low:
Praise him who is great with a lift of our plates!

Our God gives pumpkin pie, my boys,
Our God gives pumpkin pie!

Thanks For Ever

"But as for me, I am like a green olive-tree in the house of
God: I trust in the lovingkindness of God for ever and
ever. I will give thee thanks for ever, because thou hast
done it; And I will hope in thy name, for it is good, in the
presence of thy saints."
Psalm 52:8, 9

I. Taking Time

Why do we mark out special time,
and why do we mark it with food, and with rhyme?
The Lordship of Christ's in all of history,
He enacts it through means, both obvious and mystery.
This poem's about good Jesus, our King,
And how he has made us right able to sing
Thanksgiving to him throughout the whole year
For taking away all our dooms and our fears.

This poem might get complicated,
So I'll explain how it's all related.

Adam was put in a garden sweet,
Where the fruit of the ground was sufficient meat.
All of the earth was his domain,
Even time was beneath his reign.
For God had made him not to die,
With eternal life beneath the sky.

But when we sinned we began to fear,
As seasons turn then death draws near.
Where once time meant more life with God,

Now time stalked, and ripped, and clawed.
The pagan man felt the trap of age,
That time and death were a bitter cage.
So Norseman, Greek, and the Chinese,
Said time was a circle, with no surcease.
The seasons and time would go ever round,
And crush all our cities to powder fine-ground.

Then Jesus came to make the world new,
The circle was broken, time was made true.
While earth and the seasons still cycle and spin,
Time marches toward her first goal in the end.
Creation anew, which came and which comes,
Brought a sense of time to his new Chosen Ones.
He's called us to climb up to his holy hill,
Sing thanks that he's saved us, is saving us still!

We now mark the year as Christians may,
By festival, feast, and by high holy day.
A humble spirit and grateful heart
For the spiritual food that He does impart.
This poem next will tell who hears,
Thanksgiving ends and begins the year
With gratitude for all his provender
As it opens and ends the Christian calendar.

II. *The Holiday*

Thanksgiving comes in autumn time,
which is the time of fading.
The glory of the trees is gone
and winter soon comes raiding.

And death has stalked us all for long;
death will still come creeping.
In winter man has need for bread,
and hunger finds him weeping.

In spring man watches skies for rain
and knows his life is set
On whether earth will grant reward
for labor and for sweat.

In summer all begins to grow,
the beasts and the diseases.
If death can close its awful jaw,
it never will release us.

And so the world will spin its course;
Adam counts the seasons.
The sons of Adam never make
escape, by force or reason.

But Jesus made the world brand new
when Jesus broke the ages.
Time had trapped us in a ring;
we now ascend, in stages.

We once were caught by time and death,
the seasons were our prison.
Now we climb the Holy Mount,
and sing that he is risen.

Now songs are what will mark our time
as we climb to be near.
Thanksgiving Day can summon us
to sing a festal year.

Thanksgiving comes in autumn time,
which is the time of reaping.
The glory of the fruit lives on
for the food that we are keeping
To feast and drink when Advent brings
Heaven's Bread to the table.
Winter comes, but we are warmed
by Creation in a stable.

All the beasts and all the nations!
They all may enter the store.
The winter brings Epiphany,
and nations stream up to the door.

Within that door the seed is kept,
At Easter it will flourish.
We the buried all rise up,
With manna we are nourished.

The fruit of summer rises up
in the time we named Ordinary.
Where once was jungle, now we find
Garden, farm, and dairy.

From there our summer leads to fall,
we've been fed from day to day.
A year has cycled fully 'round,
We sang ascent up heaven's way.

On Advent Sunday another year
will be marked out in song,
where every Sunday's a holy day
and festal weeks are long.

This new creation and new time
is a joy to the grateful.
We thank our God, who did provide
down to every plateful.

So this is where our verse can change,
and cheer our celebration.
America may thank our God,
the Church is his true nation.

Our fathers found, in hostile land,
an unexpected mercy.
And so do we, and just like they,
we feast upon a turkey!

So let us thank the one true God
for good gifts and for plenty.
Begin this year, now raise a cheer
in thanks to One for many.

III. Thanksgiving For The Turkey

We thank our God for the turkey who died,
For farmers from Georgia, and peanut oil.
It's fairly good baked, but it's better deep-fried
In a pot full of fat that's been brought to a boil.

These orange potatoes, which some have called sweet,
Were never named thus by we honest fellows.
To live up to their name, to be proper and meet,
We've added brown sugar, and also marshmallows.

We thank God for beer, this strong heady ale,
With which we toast health, and might come from Him.
Yes, sugar and yeast make beer hearty and hale,
As the wine of the Spirit gives vigor and vim.

So here is good health to the people of God
Who love him in every season and day.
For He loved us first, which seems a bit odd,
But now we're his children, so hip-hip...hooray!

We children will toast our great God, who is Father.
Mighty hen, we're his chicks, in his bosom we lay.
Creator of all, our Good Guide and our Rudder,
Sustains us each day, so hip-hip...hooray!

Again, let us cheer our strong God, who is Son.
Came down from Heaven, so that He may
Conquer our death, a fight that he won.
He's the first-fruits of life, so hip-hip...hooray!

Once more we'll cheer our swift God, who is Spirit.
He's given to us, and with us He'll stay.
A comfort, a joy, whenever we're wearied,
He'll never forsake us, so hip-hip...hooray!

So now raise your glasses, and encourage your neighbor,
With Thanksgiving cheer the God who gives favor!

To Father, Son, and Holy Spirit, let's drink our thanks!

ABOUT THE AUTHOR

Joffre Swait is very tall, pretty dark, and kind of handsome. He lives in the upcountry of South Carolina with his wife and five children, in a modest house with a beautiful garden. He makes his living teaching Spanish, Portuguese, and English as a second language. He is more ambivalent about the Norman invasion than Tolkien was. He is co-author of *Christian Pipe-Smoking: An Introduction to Holy Incense* with Uri Brito.

Joffre is around the social media as Joffre The Giant. He can be found on YouTube at www.youtube.com/joffrethegiant and blogs at www.joffrethegiant.blogspot.com.

You can find more books from Jovial Press at www.jovial-pub.com.

www.ingramcontent.com/pod-product-compliance
Lightning Source LLC
Chambersburg PA
CBHW031630040426
42452CB00007B/760